Acknowledgements

The authors would like to recognize the following members of the Colorado Department of Education for their support in reviewing and editing this manual:

Phillip Wilson
Carol Kightlinger
Anjanette Mapp

Additionally, the authors would like to acknowledge the many teachers and related services staff who have taken the time and energy to provide feedback to this document.

Individualizing Learner Outcomes:

Infusing Student Needs into the Regular Education Curriculum

In response to the call for national educational reform, a growing number of states, including Colorado, are adopting policies focusing on the restructuring of schools to define and achieve quality education for all students through standards-driven education. Based on the fundamental belief that "all children can and must learn at ever higher levels" (National Council on Education Standards and Training, 1992) these policies are aimed at promoting equity, improving student learning and reinforcing accountability of school systems. In Colorado, education reform is focusing on development of clear content standards and implementation of an assessment process inclusive of all students. It will serve as an important starting point and framework for efforts to improve education in Colorado.

Until recently, educational reform focused solely on improved student outcomes for the typical range of learners in the regular education classroom (Giangreco, 1992). However, the movement toward inclusive education for learners with disabilities within the regular education classroom has generated a need to extend the view of these restructuring activities. The impetus toward educating all students within their neighborhood school and grade-appropriate classroom will require learning experiences which respect and reflect the range of interests, learning abilities, ethnic and cultural backgrounds, and lifelong goals of each of its students. Further, as schools shift toward inclusive educational practices, they will be required to determine methods which address the unique and individualized needs of learners with disabilities within the regular education setting.

Therefore, the success of educating all students with disabilities, including those with the most significant support needs, within regular education environments will be dependent upon how educators problem-solve ways for students to express their learning. The techniques used to evaluate and address the child's unique learning and support needs within the context of the day to day curricular activities and classroom routines will be critical for maximal student participation. With appropriate and systematic measurement, thoughtful planning and ongoing problem solving, educators can determine individual outcomes of learning for students who will require adjustments to their school experiences.

This manual has been developed in an attempt to provide educators with a process to integrate the life-long goals and specific needs of students with the most severe disabilities within the context of the regular education curriculum through the development of individualized learner outcomes. It is our sincere hope that these strategies will benefit readers in the creation of optimal learning opportunities for any student who will require adjustments to the regular education curriculum to meet their diverse learning abilities.

Building Inclusive Learning Opportunities

As skilled and dedicated educators throughout Colorado team together to provide quality inclusive services to all students, there will be a need to problem-solve and value the variety of ways students can demonstrate their learning abilities within the foundations of the regular education curriculum. The array of learners in inclusive classrooms will acquire and apply knowledge at different levels and rates (Udvari-Solner, 1993). Schools that respect the educational needs of individual learners seek to ensure that all students' lives are improved as a result of having participated in public schooling. Moreover, these student-centered schools address the life-long goals of each learner by furnishing experiences which will enhance the gifts and talents of each while building the necessary skills to achieve these goals. Indeed, the richness of the general education curriculum provides opportunities for learning which cannot be addressed in isolated settings or separate curriculum. Therefore, understanding each student's needs, accommodating their specific educational require-

ments, and expanding the network of stakeholders to problem-solve can assist schools to achieve a comprehensive and successful education for all students (Villa and Thousand 1991).

Often, educator expectations regarding the outcomes of learning activities or the way these activities are completed must be adjusted to ensure all students' successful learning of important skills. For some children and young adults who have diverse learning abilities and unique support needs, participation in all facets of school life will require team planning and problem-solving to maximize learning opportunities. Further, how teachers organize their classroom to influence and support learning must be analyzed so that educators can structure appropriate curricular activities for students who may need to learn different or additional skills to achieve their life goals.

There are two significant and inter-dependent elements which interact throughout the learning process: classroom instruction and student performance. Student performance is directly dependent on the instruction and curricular activities that occur within regular education settings. The

success of instruction is measured by the student's ability to apply learned information to actual experiences and activities within the classroom setting and real-life situations. When the expectations within classroom curriculum, instruction, and routines are congruent with the individual student goals, learning style and needs, students can typically apply learned skills across a variety of situations with little or no supports. However, where the learner's performance differs due to discrepant goals, learning style, abilities and needs, the performance expectations of the activity may need to be supported, adapted, or altered.

Traditional assessment of student learning, including norm or criteria-referenced formal assessments, may not be practical or useful in providing educators with information about student preferences, interests, abilities, and instructional needs. Therefore, a useful process for educators will be to gather information about the individual student's lifelong goals, learning support needs, and classroom curriculum and instruction in an effort to identify outcomes of the learning process which will maximize student performance. Additionally, educators must provide multiple opportunities to demonstrate their learning progress in settings that are as close to real-life settings as possible (Armstrong, 1994).

What are Learner Outcomes?

The global expectations of providing a public education for all students is to prepare them to be contributing adult members within a heterogeneous society. An array of skills, necessary for adult life functioning, are infused within classroom routines and curricular activities. Development of these skills will assist students in areas such as future employment, home and self care, relationships, money management, lifelong learning, and community access. There are expectations of how students will demonstrate their learning of these skills within the classroom routines and curriculum. These defined expectations of performance are often referred to as learner outcomes. Learner outcomes provide teachers with a reference to evaluate student mastery of the skills and abilities defined by the curriculum and instructional practices. Therefore, a critical and initial task in defining expecta-

tions of any learning environment is to consider the specific learner outcomes expected of the student (Bellamy, 1993).

To illustrate this process, consider the activities of a fifth grade social studies class. A learning goal defined for this grade student is "to identify the location of countries with respect to the United States and have an awareness of the critical trade exports of each." School building teams or individual teachers may discern student mastery of this goal might include locating and displaying materials regarding foreign trade, labeling continents and countries, explaining import/export, and identifying, at a minimum, ten countries with which the United States trades and the major commodities exchanged. The different instructional strategies and classroom management techniques used may require that students work in groups, access the library, self-monitor daily progress, and present oral and/or written presentation of projects to classmates.

Examples of typical learner outcomes for this 5th grade social studies class

might look like this:

- locate and research materials regarding foreign trade
- label major continents and countries
- explain import/export
- identify ten countries with which the United States trades and the major commodities exchanged.
- participate as a team member in a cooperative group
- track personal work completed on a weekly monitor sheet
- give an oral presentation and written report on three foreign countries and trades

Why are Learner Outcomes Important?

Learner outcomes provide a day to day framework for measuring student knowledge and growth in curricular content areas. Moreover, learner outcomes give the student a general idea of teacher expectations as well a guide for setting personal goals. Identifying learner outcomes can also assist teachers with monitoring student progress toward understanding and integrating the knowledge defined by the curriculum, knowing and following classroom routines and rules, as well as indicating a student's need for corrective feedback and further instruction. Although most students will be able to demonstrate mastery of these learner outcomes to some degree, students with diverse learning abilities will require varying types and amounts of instructional supports. Further, learners with diverse abilities and significant support needs may require alternative or adapted learner outcomes which reference the same skill area to successfully enable them to participate to the fullest extent within regular education settings. Although some students may have difficulty performing skills within activities defined to achieve typical learner outcomes, they may be able to learn and perform different levels of proficiencies which demonstrate their growth toward the content area.

Consider the previous example which identifies the learner outcomes for a social studies class. A student who has diverse learning abilities and significant support needs may not be able to read materials and communicate information through typical class discussion or writing activities necessary for performance demonstration. However, the student can show an awareness of the global trade economy through performance of alternative communication and written language proficiencies within the same classroom activities. The typical learner outcomes can be altered or adapted to allow the student to perform similar proficiencies such as:

✎ listen to taped reading materials which explain major products of those countries
✎ learn the names of two different countries
✎ draw pictures which illustrate export/import products
✎ match pictures of products to corresponding countries on map.
✎ participate as a team member in a cooperative group
✎ color in completed assignment on monitoring sheet
✎ word process one paragraph of information about a foreign country from encyclopedia and have peer audiotape for class presentation

To ensure all students have opportunities to learn and demonstrate their learning of the curriculum, it is important to be thoughtful about how to infuse the learner's unique and individual instructional and support needs within the daily curriculum and instruction. Creating alternative ways for students to utilize their unique strengths and abilities to demonstrate their learning is as important as understanding the unique support and instructional needs of students who have diverse abilities. To effectively identify individualized learner outcomes which reflect student lifelong learning goals, strengths, preferences, and instructional needs, a systematic process to understand the student's needs and ability to perform skills in various settings will be useful. Steps within this systematic process include:

1. Identify the learner's lifelong goals and aptitudes for school and community participation

2. Determine instructional needs and/or supports to maximize the learner's participation in curricular activities or routines

3. Analyze the classroom routines and activities to determine typical learner outcomes students are expected to demonstrate

Step 1—Identify the learner's lifelong goals and aptitudes for school and community participation.	Step 2—Determine the instructional needs and supports to maximize the learner's participation in curricular activities or routines.	Step 3—Analyze the classroom routines and activities to determine typical learner outcomes.	Step 4—Observe and determine the learner's ability to perform typical learner outcomes.	Step 5—Identify individualized learner outcomes which reflect the curricular content focus and the learner's lifelong goals and instructional needs.
Questions to ask: *Who is this learner?* • What is the history of this student? • What does this student like? • What are this student's abilities and strengths? • What physical supports and/or accommodations are necessary for this student? *What are the learner's dreams?* • What future education/career goals do this student and family have? • Where will this student live? • What are this student's abilities and strengths? • Who will be in the student's social network? *What are the learner's nightmares?* • What does this student and his/her family fear will happen in the future if supports are not provided? *Assessment to Use* Individualized Planning Strategies	**Questions to ask:** *What will the student need to participate in school?* • What skills will the student need to learn? • What physical supports and modifications need to be available? • What information will the regular education teacher need to adjust instruction, individualize curriculum, and/or modify the physical structure of the classroom? *Assessment to Use* Checklist for Identifying Student Support and Instructional Needs within Regular Education Classrooms **Questions to ask:** *Across the student's day, what activities/enviroments offer opportunities to develop the skills and receive the supports previously identified?* *Assessment to Use* Daily Schedule/Student Needs Matrix	**Questions to ask:** *What are the expectations in classroom routines and activities?* • What are the curricular objectives of this class/course? • What are the typical routines and activities used to achieve the outcome? • How is information presented? • What learning materials are used? • How are grades determined? *Assessment to Use* Classroom/Course Analysis **Questions to ask:** *What are the typical learner outcomes within these routines and activities?* • What is the sequence of steps necessary to perform the activity? • How do classmates perform these steps? *Assessment to Use* Student Observation Form Class Routine/Curricular Sequence	**Questions to ask:** *Can the student perform the typical learner outcome?* • What steps does the learner perform independently? • What steps does the learner need instructional support to perform? • What steps will require adaptations, different materials, or physical support to perform? • What outcomes will need to be altered so that the student can demonstrate a similar performance? • Will the student require an alternative curriculum activity at this time? *Assessment to Use* Student Observation Form Student Level of Participation	**Questions to ask:** *Where the student is unable to perform the typical learner outcome, what outcomes can they perform which will maximize their participation in the curricular activity and address instructional needs?* • Do the curricular objectives relate to the student's lifelong goals? • Can the student perform the outcome with adapted materials or physical assistance? • Are there similar skills the student can perform which reflect instructional needs and relate to the curricular content? • If the student is unable to perform the same, similar or adapted outcome, are there alternative activities based upon identified needs which can be worked on during that time? *Assessment to Use* Individualized Learner Outcome Matrix

Table I

4. Observe and determine the learner's to ability perform typical learner outcomes

5. Identify individualized Learner outcomes which reflect the curricular content focus and the learner's life long goals and instructional needs

Table I provides an inquiry framework to complete each of these five steps, including the questions to ask during each phase of this process and the assessment tools which may be useful when gathering data to answer these questions. To provide learners with educational experiences which meet their unique needs and prepare them for adult life, it will be important to understand the goals of each child or youth. The initial step in this process, then, is to gain insight about the student as an individual.

Step 1:

Identify the learner's lifelong goals and aptitudes for school and community participation

> *Who is this learner?*
> *What are the learner's dreams?*
> *What are the learner's fears?*

Student lifelong goals

At one time or another during our childhood, we all imagined what our life would be like when we became older. We dreamed about what we would be when we grew up, where we might live, and who our friends might be. Several of us made plans and achieved them early on in adulthood. Some of us shifted our life goals many times during our pursuit of our dreams. And a few of us did not recognize our strengths and abilities at an early age, and so became "late bloomers". For example, not many of us were told we would be good teachers by those who were instructing us during our school years. One role of educators has typically been to help children recognize their strengths, abilities, and poten-

tial, as well as provide them with opportunities to explore their dreams. This is especially important when planning with and for students who have significantly diverse learning abilities.

Many students and their families have expectations of school experiences. Each student and their family, however, may value and desire very different outcomes of education for adult life. Therefore, viewing the learner and their family as equal contributors to the educational process is critical to effective planning. A common understanding of the learner's goals and the family's goals for the student's future will assist educators in determining what skills students will need to reach their dreams. Additionally, such an understanding will help determine what supports students may need to fully realize their ambitions, and develop the interests, strengths, and abilities that reinforce their life directions.

There are different methods for determining such goals. Some educators may be familiar with such recognized techniques as Making Action

Plans (Falvey, Forest, Pearpoint, & Rosenberg, 1994) and Personal Futures Planning (Mount, 1987). Across Colorado, a similar process known as Individualized Planning Sessions (IPS), (Roggow & Connolly, 1992), which incorporates these various techniques, has been effective in bringing key players in the education of students with significant support needs together to focus on the present and future plans of the individual. Students, their families and peers, as well as the educators and others involved in the student's life collaborate to understand the learner's lifelong ambitions as well as determine ways to support the realization of these goals.

There are several end results that can be realized when using this strategy. One such outcome is the creation of a student-centered planning team. A student-centered planning team is a group of individuals who problem-solve and plan together to create an optimal educational experience for individual students who may require different or additional supports and instruction within the regular education classroom. This team can include any combination of individuals, such as teachers, parents, therapists, students, etc., who collaborate together to ensure the instruction, adaptations, and physical supports needed to meet the student's lifelong goals identified through the IPS are provided.

The IPS promotes a structured person-centered process for the recognition of student and family dreams. Additionally, this process results in the development of an action planning system for achieving connections within the student's school and community environments. IPS allows participants to crystallize their vision for the learner as they facilitate educational planning, allowing for a more meaningful vehicle for collaboration. Moreover, including the learner, their family, and other's significant in the child's life as part of the planning team can ensure respect of student decisions while expanding the array of problem-solvers. The essential elements of an IPS process include:

- honoring family values through their active participation

- incorporating dreaming and planning in a positive, supportive process
- utilizing jargon-free language
- focusing on student strengths and gifts
- including the student and his/her friends in the planning process
- promoting open and guilt-free communication
- providing visual illustrations of pertinent information

As schools begin to address the unique characteristics and needs of each individual student within inclusive settings, IPS is a valuable tool which can interface directly with the Individualized Education Program (IEP). The IPS is a participant-friendly way to assist with identifying support needs, setting goals to address those needs, and encouraging collaborative, problem-solving efforts between participants. Families and educators choose to be involved in an IPS (or other person-centered planning process) in order to utilize a vehicle which is more interactive for the participants and emphasizes the value of families. The focus on student strengths and needs, with respect to their lifelong learning goals, allows the planning team to brainstorm and provide support as the student and his/her family become empowered to participate in their school and home communities. This person-centered strategy can be key towards the building of relationships for the learner within their school and general community.

In the IPS process, the student and their family, together with friends, teachers, and other persons significant in their life, come together to address questions which allow the group to understand the reality of the student's world. A sample of some of the questions from the IPS menu might include:

Who is the learner?
What are our dreams for the learner?
What are our fears for the learner?
What are the learner's gifts?
What works/what does not work for the learner?
What is the current schedule for this learner?
What does an "ideal day" look like for the learner?

What will the learner need to maximize his/her participation within this schedule?

The IPS process facilitates the understanding of who the student is in terms of his/her gifts and needs, what the dreams and fears might be for the child and his/her family, and what a typical day might look like for this student. IPS also can focus members of the student-centered planning teams to identify specific supports/resources that can assist the student in increasing school and community connections. Additional outcomes realized through IPS have included: familiarizing all participants with the needs of the individual student so that everyone is on "equal ground"; answering questions about "Where do we go from here?"; increasing the number of environments in which the student is a participant; expanding the vision for the student; and expanding the quality of life for the student through increased choices, empowerment and by altering the way the learner is viewed.

IPS can build the foundation for a mutual and respectful decision-making process within the student-centered planning team. Moreover, this student-focused strategy can set the stage for planning teams to jointly identify and plan for the personal supports students will require to meet their individual needs within the regular education setting.

To assist with illustrating this process, consider the following case study:

Phillip is a 9-year-old young man who will be attending Forrest Heights Elementary School in the fall. He's a happy and loving child who has an excellent self-image and a strong will. His friends describe him as funny, playful, and silly. They also comment on how much he enjoys coming to their houses to play. His parents state that Phillip is a caring, lively, and sometimes stubborn child. Phillip has Down Syndrome, but is like typical nine-year-olds in his strengths and interests. His parents want him to have experiences similar to those of other fourth graders. That is why Phillip's parents have requested that he attend his neighborhood school and grade-appropriate classroom in the fall.

Phillip attended preschool at a community-centered board program for children with disabilities and began his public education in a self-contained classroom within a local elementary school (not his neighborhood school). However, his family, friends, classmates and teachers have all seen the benefits to Phillip of being involved with his same age peers through integration into specials and some academic

Figure 2
Who is Phillip?

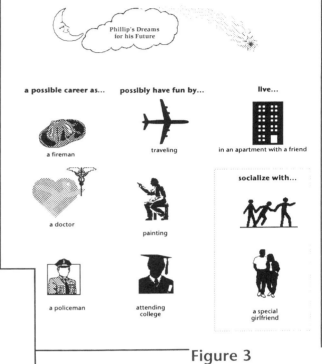

Figure 3
Phillip's Dreams

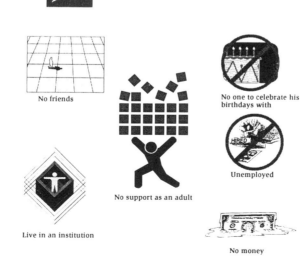

Figure 4
Phillip and His Family's Fears

9

classes. He models his peers and enjoys the friendships that he has established within the center-based school and within his neighborhood. Therefore, his parents have decided that inclusion into the attendance area school could increase Phillip's social, academic, and life-skills growth.

The educational team supporting Phillip must now decide how to interface Phillip's lifelong goals and learning needs within the fourth grade curriculum. They have decided that an Individualized Planning Session would provide critical information about Phillip and his educational needs. The educational team, including his family, friends, past and current teachers, have all come together and have gathered information about him (*Figures 2–4*).

Step 2:

Determine the instructional needs and/or supports to maximize the learner's participation in curricular activities or routines

What will the student need to participate in school?

We all have individual ways in which we gather, process, use, and relate information from our environments as we learn to attain our lifelong goals. Knowing our unique learning and communication characteristics aides us in performing at our best as we participate in activities at work, home, or play. Individualized Planning Sessions allow educational teams to identify the lifelong goals of individual students, as well as activities which will assist them with gaining their dreams. While IPS addresses some needs of the student and can identify some general supports to assist the learner, a more systematic process to determine student needs within specific environments will be necessary. In an effort to maximize the benefits of those academic, social, and life-skills learning opportunities, it will be important for student-centered planning teams to determine the general skills and supports which students will need, as a result of their diverse learning abilities, to participate in these activities. Analysis of these skills and support needs include those skills and supports which are critical in any environment the student is in and those which increase access to activities and routines within school settings.

To identify a student's support and instructional needs, planning teams must consider the environmental and curricular considerations, based on the unique, individual learner characteristics, which are critical to the student's ability to participate in any environment they are in. Additionally, teams will need to determine those skills which will require planned and systematic instruction for the learner to achieve life goals through active learning within classroom activities and routines. These considerations for skill development and supports include the learner's:

- communicative intent, abilities and methods
- behavioral and/or affective considerations
- assistance or accommodation needs
- social interactions and relationship needs
- personal care and organization
- time management abilities
- academically-related task performance
- life-skill development

Understanding the Communicative Needs of the Learner

Using communication to interact with others in our life is necessary to get our basic needs met and to establish and build relationships with others. Some learners may use alternative communication methods such as picture systems, sign language, or eye-blinking to indicate their wants or needs. Some students may rely on methods other than verbal language to communicate. For instance, rather than asking for a crayon which another student may have, the learner might grab the teachers arm to indicate his/her want to attain that color crayon. This interactive process is known as communicative intent (Donnellan, Mirenda, Mesaros, & Fassbender, 1984).

To maximize the student's learning, it is important for educators to understand the communicative intent of learners who may use different communication methods and to provide opportunities for students to interact using different, or replacement, methods. The student who grabs the teacher to indicate a want for a crayon might be taught to signal a need for assistance by tapping the teacher's shoulder and pointing to a picture of the desired object. Teacher modeling of effective interactions with the student who uses alternative communication methods can be used to instruct classmates and facilitate subsequent relationships. Moreover, respecting and validating the learner's communicative intent, abilities and methods can promote self-advocacy skills for present and future assistance needs.

To effectively address the learner's communicative intent, abilities and methods, student-centered teams will need to consider the typical communication interactions within classroom activities and routines when planning for each student. Communication expectations of students may vary depending on grade-level, activity, and instructional setting. Typical expectations of student communication may include such interactions as:

- initiating/responding to greetings
- participating in classroom discussions
- requesting assistance
- sharing ideas and suggestions

When planning for critical communication supports, teams should consider the following factors which influence successful interactions for each student:

- student access to usable and portable communication methods and/ or systems which are responsive to inherent communication interactions within classroom activities
- teacher and classmate awareness and understanding of the learner's communication methods
- student need for direct instruction to use the communication method/system
- opportunities for the student to practice and use the communication method/system within classroom activities
- teacher and classmate validation of the learner's communication

Many students have limited or informal means of communicating their wants and needs. In the past, individuals supporting students with significant needs did not recognize such challenges as relating to communication; rather, they perceived the challenges as behavioral issues. The student who had a temper tantrum because she could not have access to the water fountain was merely seen as exhibiting non-compliant behavior. The most current approaches, however, suggest that we provide support for increasing and enhancing a variety of modes of communication in order to decrease behavioral outbursts.

Understanding the Behavioral and/or Affective Needs of the Student

All behavior occurs for a reason (Haring & Lovinger, 1989). Understanding why some students act out can assist educators to cope with and support learners who may require environmental/curricular adaptations and/or alternative instructional strategies to support their learning in the general education environment. If the appropriate supports for the student are put in place in a proactive manner, the likelihood of the student's acting out can be decreased significantly. Effective classroom structure and management is key to developing a successful learning environment. The establishment of routines, rules,

and natural consequences can provide all children and young adults with structures to teach and maintain expected classroom behavior. However, even with the most skillful utilization of preventative techniques, there may be some learners who will benefit from approaches to support behavioral change which are in addition to or different from typical classroom management structures.

Further, there may be students who will require direct instruction to use a replacement for unacceptable behaviors as their method of communication. Remember the example of the student who grabbed the teacher because he/she wanted a crayon. This student could not vocalize his/her need, but used grabbing to get the teacher attention. Planned and structured instruction must be scheduled to teach the leaner a more desirable method of signaling the need for teacher assistance. Therefore, in order to teach a student different behaviors, it will be critical for student-centered planning teams to understand the motivation of a student to act in ways that are usually considered inappropriate or disruptive.

Understanding the motivation can also assist the planning teams in setting long-term educational goals and providing instructional strategies which address the affective and behavioral needs of the student. Consider ways in which students may gain the teacher's attention during a class discussion. Some children may raise their hands quietly and wait for the teacher to call upon them; others may call out the teacher's name while getting out of their seats. Some may grab at the teacher, as in the previous example. All of these methods may be effective in gaining the teachers attention. However, raising hands to answer questions may be the classroom rule or the teacher's desired method for students to gain attention.

A crucial task of team members, then, is to determine why a learner acts in what is considered as an inappropriate manner and what skills the student will need to learn to get the desired outcome in an appropriate, yet effective way. Some elements which influence how students respond within the classroom structure include the following:

- communication of expected behaviors during each activity
- feedback provided to learners regarding their behavior
- type of consequences and immediacy of employment
- ways in which positive behavior is regarded
- consequences for negative behavior

When planning for critical behavioral and/or affective skill development and supports, teams should consider the following factors which can influence successful classroom instruction for each student:

- teacher proximity to the student during instructional activities
- level of prompting and reinforcement required by the learner to maintain successful performance
- ability of the student to use self-management techniques, including self-directed goal setting and self-monitoring of behaviors
- student's need for instruction in appropriate replacement behaviors
- teacher understanding and use of redirective techniques

- availability of choices within activities
- activities of interest, ability, and motivation for student

Understanding the Physical Support Needs of the Learner

At one time or another, we all need a "little help from our friends." So too, some learners with diverse needs may require physical assistance from friends or adults to participate in all aspects of the classroom activities. Different mobility and movement abilities of individuals may require peer or teacher support for students to move from one area to another or to turn pages of a workbook. Given their physical needs, some students may perform better if they are allowed to stand or lay rather than sit in a chair for an extended period of time. Others may require the placement of materials within different visual fields to adequately see their work. Further, some learners may need alternative seating positions during the day to ensure their comfort and physical well-being.

Planned environmental alterations, as well as personal assistance through peer support, can increase the learner's opportunities to access all classroom routines and activities. Checking to make sure the areas the learner participates in are barrier free can help to ensure a safer classroom for all students. Furthermore, all students benefit through learning how to help each other. Teams should assess how each learner's physical needs will be addressed within the typical physical requirements of classroom activities and routines. Some of the classroom environmental conditions or typical physical requirements which may require team attention include:

- physical setup of the classroom
- available space within areas where instruction takes place
- physical positions of students and duration of activities
- fine motor skills used within activities such as cutting, writing, stapling, etc.
- materials frequently utilized
- movement during hall passing periods
- proximity of classmates for assistance

When planning for critical physical needs and supports, teams should consider the following factors which influence successful classroom access for each student:

- ✐ mobility assistance needs of the student
- ✐ physical activity requirements of the student
- ✐ student seating arrangement needs
- ✐ physical ability of the student to manipulate materials and technology needs
- ✐ student workspace needs
- ✐ classmate availability for support

Understanding the Social Interaction and Relationship Needs of the Learner

All humans have the basic need for love and belonging (Maslow, 1968). Forming mutually-valuing relationships can achieve the meeting of that need. By nature of their function, schools offer limitless opportunities for the development of these relationships. For the child who is socially adept and outgoing, the task of forming friendships comes naturally. However, some children and youth remain isolated due to lack of awareness and skills to form those relationships in a mutually acceptable manner. Learners who have different communication modes and/or learning abilities than their peers may require direct instruction to appropriately initiate or respond in interactions with others. Further, classmates, educators, and personnel within the school may need to have interactions with the student modeled for them to understand the communicative intent and style or affective needs of the student.

Knowing how children and young adults of different age levels gain and maintain friendships is important in an effort to determine how to best support each student with relationship development. Schools are typically rich environments where social development of children can be enhanced. However, some students may not understand how to go about gaining and/or maintaining a positive relationship with their peers. Therefore, many educators have incorporated prosocial skill activities as part of the daily social studies curriculum to encourage the growth of healthy interactions. Additionally, some school communities have found the use of schoolwide governance structures helps to foster friendships among their children and also encourages a cooperative climate within the building. Whenever we can share in the notion that everyone (students and adults) can learn how to get along better, the burden to change becomes less on the child who is experiencing difficulties. Many times, simply changing the environment fosters the nurturing that's needed. Recent studies have found that a school's support and nurturing of the growth of relationships among its students and faculty is a critical factor in bringing about school change (Sergiovanni, 1994).

Relationships between children and young adults at different grade levels may be influenced by an array of factors. Often, their physical proximity in activities will facilitate the growth of relationships between primary-aged children. Youth at the intermediate level may come together around common interests, such as sports or preferred entertainment activities. Since the way relationships are formed alter throughout a student's educational experiences, teams should examine the social culture at each grade level and across grade levels. When observing children busy in social interactions, educators should look to see how the following areas are integrated:

- verbal and nonverbal communication used to initiate interactions
- typical conversational topics
- length of interactions
- common expressions used
- activities which stimulate interest
- proximity of children to each other during conversations, classroom tasks, and playground activities
- ways in which interactions are brought to closure

When identifying the specific skills and designing the supports which students may require to develop and/or maintain mutual friendships, educational teams should be sensitive to the following:

- student communication abilities
- preferred activities and/or talents of the student
- student-demonstrated preference for certain classmates
- classmate and school staff need for modeling of interactions

- naturally-occurring opportunities for interactions between classmates
- least intrusive methods to facilitate interactions between the student and his/her classmates

Understanding the Personal Care and Organization Needs of the Learner

Given the nature of their structure, schools are often places where children begin to learn how to manage their personal needs and assume responsibility for organizing their materials and space in an effective an efficient manner. As they become older, children are expected to assume more control for their own personal needs without the schedules or reminders provided to younger learners. Further, the types of personal needs attended to during the school day may change as students move from level to level. Additionally, personal organizers, which assist students to structure themselves, such as assignment notepads, classroom cubbies, etc., may change at different grade levels.

Therefore, it will be necessary for individual planning team members to address the variety of personal care and organizational demands and structures evident at each grade level. Some components of these may include, but not be limited to:

- personal care needs at each grade level
- times of the day students attend to personal care needs
- time spent on personal care
- location of restrooms, drinking fountains to classroom
- organization of personal belongings (e.g. in desk or locker)
- number of times throughout the day do students usually access lockers
- materials needed to keep personal belongings organized (e.g. school box, notebook tabs)

When identifying the specific skills and determining the supports which students may require to attend to personal care needs and organization, educational teams should consider the following:

- ability of the student to communicate personal assistance needs
- personal style preferences of each student

- physical assistance needs of the student
- mobility abilities of the student

Understanding the Time Management Needs of the Learner

Occasionally, there isn't enough time to achieve what we had hoped to accomplish in a certain period. Learning how to effectively manage our time is an easy task for some, and difficult for others. Pacing ourselves and "watching the clock" are skills many of us have learned to predict our time needs. However, some of us may require adaptations in our daily lives to assist with monitoring task completion and time management. Some of these adaptations may include a daytimer calendar, watch, and/or alarm clock. To be sure, pacing ourselves throughout the day by following a routine and anticipating time needs are skills required throughout our lives.

Prioritizing our activities and completing them within given time periods are skills most of us learn early in school. These skills are embedded in the typical daily routines and demands within the classroom and school environments. Conforming to these time standards provides a structure for students to anticipate activity changes and gage the sequence of events involved in the daily routine. Although internalizing schedules and routines, as well as effectively managing time to complete daily activities is a skill that many children learn within the first years of school, some learners with diverse abilities may require intentional instruction and adaptations around time management.

To ensure appropriate instruction in these areas, teams will need to evaluate typical time management requirements within the school setting, including but not limited to knowing:

- typical daily schedules of the grade level
- cues available to let students know when activities are changing
- time allotment for transition from activity to activity
- room or teacher changes throughout the day
- hallway activity during class period changes
- consequences for tardiness

As teams come together to plan for the necessary instruction to promote student interdependence within the school and future settings, the following information may prove useful for effective instructional planning:

- classmate availability for mobility assistance
- ability of student to self-monitor time
- ability of student to attend to natural cues and/or need for object, picture, or written schedule
- time factors associated with mobility methods
- need for transition preparation

Understanding the Academic Needs of the Learner

An important educational outcome for all students is the acquisition of the skills and knowledge necessary to be a contributing member of the community. The school curriculum is designed to reflect the content each community values as necessary for learners to become "educated" members. Presentation of the regular school curriculum is purposeful to provide information for the development, acquisition, and maintenance of these skills. Each content area has an outcome identified for application to life activities. For instance, the outcome of teaching content in language arts is thought to be the building of skills necessary for students to competently express themselves through written and oral language methods.

For most students, this outcome is easily achieved through mastery and application of the regular curricular content to a wide array of written and spoken formats. However, for some students with diverse learning abilities, generalization of skills to a wide variety of environments and activities may be difficult. Therefore, the design of the curriculum must be well planned and purposeful to provide the necessary instruction of academic skills in activities which are meaningful and useful to the learner, and experiences must be expanded to include all diverse learners.

To determine relevant academic skills for individual students who require more support, it will be necessary for team members to identify components within the regular curriculum, including:

- basic skills infused into curricular activities
- specific roles within cooperative learning groups to master content as well as learning how to work in group
- outcomes of curricular content
- activities used to teach curricular content
- expected performance standards to demonstrate mastery of curricular content

The educational team should consider the following for each individual student who will require additional instruction and/or supports which focus on the development and generalization of academic skills to access the regular curriculum:

- student method and ability to communicate information related to academic learning
- student application of academic skills in daily life
- ability of the student to generalize information learned from setting to setting
- motivation of the student and interest in academic content

Understanding the Life Skills Needs of the Learner

The classroom provides an array of opportunities for learning which are not directly related to academic content but are essential for students to manage themselves and the environment when they are about the business of learning. Further, these opportunities provide the foundation of skills necessary for students to participate within the home, work, and community setting as interdependent adults. These basic skills, such as following routines and keeping work areas tidy, are those skills which help to establish successful work habits for future employment. Additionally, courses such as physical education; woodworking, and home economics provide curricular content which allow students to develop an array of abilities for community participation, recreational, and interdependent living.

For the majority of students, learning and applying these basic skills to present and future settings will not be problematic. However, for a few learners who may have significantly diverse learning abilities, the initial educational focus may center primarily on the development of these skills. All environments in the school community can provide a variety of instructional experiences for students to develop, expand and practice skills for adult life participation.

Therefore, teams will need to evaluate the skills and outcomes related to the curriculum which are focused on life skills and which typical learners perform, including:

- daily routines students are expected to perform (such as selecting and paying for lunch in cafeteria, cleaning desk off each afternoon)
- specific roles within cooperative learning groups to master content as well as learning how to work in groups
- classroom jobs and/or electives designed to increase the learner's interest and responsibilities

A fter completing the Student Support/Instructional Needs Checklist and obtaining information from the IPS, Philip's team has identified the following needs within settings that he will access, including:

Communication Needs:
- respond to greetings in an age-appropriate manner
- ask for/accept teacher or peer assistance
- use a sentence to answer simplified questions during group instruction

Behavior and/or Affective Needs:
- make choices within activities
- follow directions
- attend to teacher during group instruction

Relationship Development:
- work collaboratively with classmates

Time Management:
- use a picture schedule to follow grade-level routines

Academically-Related Tasks:
- write numbers in sequence/columns

Life-Skills Development:
- dial the sequence of numbers on a telephone
- learn to use a calculator
- practice copying letters and numbers from a model (paper, board, overhead) to own paper
- increase use of technology to aid learning and recreation
- use paint as an art medium to express self
- learn about different jobs within the community

Figure 5

18

- basic skills within noncurricular activities which increase student's level of interdependent living (such as selecting food items for snack, painting woodworking creation, assisting with playtime in the preschool)

When determining the instructional needs and supports of individual students in the life skills area, teams should consider the following useful information:

✎ long-term goals of students and their families in the areas of career, domestic, recreational, and community involvement

✎ student's interests and abilities

✎ tasks that will need to be performed for students if they do not learn to do the task themselves

✎ ways in which students can partially participate in activities when they are not capable of doing the entire activity independently

Appendix A, the *Checklist for Identifying Student Support and Instructional Needs within Regular Education Classrooms*, is a tool which student-centered planning teams may incorporate to assist them in identifying the individual student instructional and support needs that students may require to enhance their membership within their grade-level classrooms. When Phillip's planning team completed the *Support/Instructional Needs Checklist*, they analyzed the information, identifying Phillip's needs across his day. The team then brainstormed the different environments in which Phillip could develop and enhance his needs (Figure 6).

Determining Where the Learner's Instructional Needs and Supports are Best Met

> *Across the student's day, what activities/environments offer opportunities for students to develop the skills and receive the supports previously identified?*

Once the needs of the student have been identified, it may be useful for teams to consider which instructional settings and curricular activities provide for the greatest opportunities for student learning. There are several benefits to incorporating this step in the assessment process. First, there may be classes or activities, based on content and/or instructional presentation, that provide greater opportunities for students to work on needed skills and/or have the necessary supports available. Second, when critical instructional periods are identified, teams can begin to arrange for specific adult supports, such as one to one instruction, personal care, etc. that will need to be scheduled. Finally, where the identified need cannot be met within the context of the grade-level schedule, alternative environment/activities within the school or community may need to be considered.

To clarify, think of a high school student who has an instructional need to use an augmentative communication system to answer questions. Drawing may not be a course where students are required to participate in much class discussion since the course focuses mostly on independent product completion. Art History, however, is a course that can accommodate both the support needs this student may require from classmates as well as planned times for the student to

Daily Schedule/Student Needs
Phillip's Classroom Schedule

Phillip's Instructional and Support Needs

	opening	spelling	gym	English	math	lunch recess	reading	specials
respond to greetings	●	●	●	●	●	●	●	●
ask/accept assistance	●	●	●	●	●	●	●	●
answer questions	●	●	●	●	●	●	●	●
make choices	●	●	●	●	●	●	●	●
follow directions	●	●	●	●	●	●	●	●
attend to teacher	●	●	●	●	●	●	●	●
work in group	●	●	●			●		
follow routine		●	●	●	●		●	●
write numbers					●			●
use telephone					●	●		
use calculator					●	●		●
copy letters from model		●		●	●		●	●
use technology		●		●	●		●	●
paint				●		●	●	●
learn about jobs					●		●	●

Figure 6

respond during group discussions. The same student may need to learn how to use public transportation to get around town. This student-centered planning team acknowledges this need cannot be addressed within any courses and will require a scheduled time for this student to receive instruction within the community. The decision to provide this support outside the regular classroom setting must be made carefully, and must be weighed with the student's need to remain with his/her peers.

In planning, then, to meet the learner's instructional and support needs within the school day, student-centered planning teams may find a matrixing process useful. Appendix B, the Daily Schedule/Student Needs Matrix, is a tool that provides student-centered teams with a visual display to list the student's schedule and needs to determine classes or activities where those needs can or cannot be sufficiently addressed. Figure 6 illustrates an example of a matrix which Phillip's team has created, infusing his support needs and curricular activities which occur throughout the day in the fourth-grade classroom. Note that there are

several activities where many of Phillip's needs can be accommodated. The team can concentrate instructional support during those activities to maximize student learning and participation.

Step 3:

Analyze the classroom routines and activities to determine typical learner outcomes students are expected to demonstrate

> **What are the classroom activity and routine expectations?**

Assessing the Classroom/Course Format

Many educators use a variety of methods to provide information to students and guide learning activities. Since teachers and their styles differ, no two teachers will present, or evaluate student's learning of the curricular content in the exact same way.

Therefore, once student-centered planning teams have completed the matrix, they will need to further assess the prioritized environments where the student's needs will be addressed. This will require team members to understand how each teacher organizes curricular activities and routines and manages instruction to facilitate student learning.

Since routines and activities which encompass the curricular content, classroom management techniques, and instructional groupings and delivery may all differ from grade level to grade level, students will be introduced to an array of learning environments. Therefore, understanding the instructional style of each teacher, content of the curriculum, and climate of the classroom can assist educators with determining where students, as well as classroom teachers, may need adaptations or supports to address the student's learning style. Observing in the classroom and collaboratively identifying the following components within the course/classroom curriculum and instruction will be useful for team members as they come together to plan for an individual student.

- expected curricular outcomes addressed; performance criteria for this class/course
- typical routines and activities used within the classroom
- style of information presentation
- grading standards
- learning materials utilized

As teams work together to problem-solve ways to maximize student participation, it will be important to focus on the learning routines, materials, expectations, and grading structures typical to the classroom. If the student will require modifications or adaptations in these areas, it will be important for teams to try to reference similar routines, management techniques, grading format, and materials.

Consider the following example:

Within a middle school classroom, students might be able to participate in a Friday party if they earn an appropriate number of points for following classroom rules throughout the week and completing all assignments.

For a student who has difficulty following all of the rules, as well as delaying gratification for five days, the team may decide fewer points will be required for this student to participate, a daily point progress sheet will be kept, and/or only one classroom rule per week will be emphasized. Referencing the typical classroom management can still hold the student accountable to follow the same behavior standards as classmates, but with modified expectations.

Teams can glean critical information about how each educator sets up their class or course through incorporating the Classroom Analysis, as provided in Appendix C, into the assessment process. Conversation with the teacher as well as observations by team members can allow student-centered planning teams to determine how student's will best operate within the general daily routines and activities of the classroom and to prepare for supports as necessary.

Remember the matrix Philip's team used to assist with identifying and prioritizing environments where his general and specific skills and support needs could be met (Figure 6)? Math class was identified as one of the instructional settings where Phillip's needs could be addressed. Mr. Ford, the teacher in the class, is a collaborative member of the planning team. Table II illustrates information gathered by the team through interviewing and observation. This knowledge lets the team know that Mr. Ford would like some assistance and modeling about how to best include Phillip and required sitting during review and instruction may be problematic if alternatives are not provided. Therefore, the team will need further information about specific student performance expectations during those activities and how Phillip accomplishes these expectations.

Classroom Analysis

Class/Course: Mathematics **Teacher:** Mr. Ford **Time Period:** 11:30 AM—12:15 PM **Room Number:** 43

What are the curricular outcomes for this class?	What is the teaching format/instructional grouping arrangement?	What are common routines/classroom management techniques?
• Students will demonstrate an understanding of basic mathematical operations and apply problem-solving strategies to everyday activities. • Students will work in small groups with shared roles to learn to evaluate, analyze, synthesize, and apply basic math operations.	Teacher does 10-minute warmup review of previous day's lesson; uses cooperative learning strategies to practice facts/functions; employs classroom games, including math bingo and fast-5, for 15 minutes daily; short didactic lecture and group boardwork to review new material, uses timed tests every week to check for accuracy and speed.	Teacher likes to stay with same schedule daily. Students quiet, in-seat during first 10–15 minutes, doing independent seatwork to copy questions from overhead, group discussion to answer problems and self-correct; move into cooperative groups for 15 minutes to review and play games; 10–15 review of new material; homework assignment followed by independent seatwork, if time. Low noise level, lots of interaction between teacher/student. Teacher uses positive reinforcement, ignores inappropriate behavior unless disruptive, then student sent out of classroom.
What learning materials are used?	**How are grades assigned?**	**What collaboration/support needs might the teacher want?**
Fourth-grade math text, paper pencil, dittos; flashcards, some use of manipulatives, will allow students to use calculator when necessary.	60% of grade is based on assignment completion and accuracy; 20% is based on weekly test scores; 10% is based on neatness of work; 10% is based on involvement in group discussion and group teaming efforts.	Teacher is open to team teaching; would like one-to-one assistance initially to model direct instruction and to strategize adaptations and learner outcomes; will allow classmate involvement if peer learning is not compromised.

Table II

Observing Classmates' Performance Within Curricular Activities

What are the typical learner outcomes within the classroom routines and activities?

How students are expected to follow classroom routines and complete activities will define the learner outcomes that progress and grades will be based on. The way a third-grader tackles an assignment to compose a story about a famous person will look different than how a high school student will complete the same assignment Further, the steps a secondary student will be expected to employ will require additional and more complex skills than a younger learner. The next phase of the assessment process, then, includes:

- observing the skills and behaviors classmates perform within routines and activities,
- determining how the teacher presents information and feedback about expected student performance, and;

This process of analyzing how a student performs within a grade-appropriate activity is frequently referred to as an ecological assessment (Brown, Hamre-Nietpski, Pumpian, Certo, & Guenewald, 1979). The information compiled in this process includes:

- typical routines and sequences of activities within the classroom;
- specific skill/behavior expectations required to perform each activity;
- instructional delivery including cues, prompts and reinforcers used; and learner performance of the skill/behavior.

To illustrate, consider a first year Spanish class at the middle school level. The curricular focus for this class includes activities which are geared toward helping students to develop understanding of Spanish-speaking cultures, to acquire new vocabulary in the language and to speak and write sentences in Spanish. Activities which help students achieve these outcomes include singing group songs in the language, learning new vocabulary through interactive discussion, and

reading stories written in the language. The beginning sequence of steps for a typical daily lesson might look like the following:

1. upon entering the room, respond to teacher's greeting and question in Spanish
2. sing a song in Spanish, demonstrating knowledge of content by following directions within the song
3. participate in game which requires responding to pictures of objects to review vocabulary
4. have small groups read chapters of stories to each other

Students gain an understanding of expected performance through instruction. Effective instruction provides students with information in the manner that they can best understand. Making sure that the student knows what skills they are to be working on, providing guided practice around these skills, and giving corrective feedback to students can increase the probability learners will attain the activity objectives, thus demonstrating the targeted learner outcomes. During the instructional process, educators impart information about expectations in a variety of ways to the students in their classroom. These teaching strategies include information provided to the learner about an expected action (cues), information provided to the learner which directs a desired response or provides feedback (prompts), and information provided to the learner which communicates his/her performance was valued and thus motivates the learner to continue the action (reinforcement).

Cues can occur naturally or can be provided through auditory, verbal, visual, and/or physical means, such as when:

- A student's stomach beings to rumble before lunch
- The school bell rings to signal the end of class
- The teacher tells his/her class to prepare for cooperative reading groups
- The teacher holds up samples to show students how their completed maps should look
- A peer physically guides a classmate to the swings on the playground

Prompts also can be delivered through verbal, gestural and/or physical means, such as:

- The teacher tells a student how to spell a word as the student writes the letters down
- A peer points to words in a book for a classmate to read in a sentence
- The teacher assistant physically guides a student's hand to form the letter "C"

Reinforcers give the student feedback about his/her actions and can be verbal, gestural, and/or physical responses, such as when:

- The teacher tells the student, "What a super job you did on this drawing!"
- The principal gives a student the thumbs-up sign for throwing away trash on the ground
- A peer gives a classmate the high-five and a clap on the back after making a goal in gym

The Spanish teacher, in the previous example, may use all of these methods to prepare the class for the day's activities. In order to assist students in achieving the learner outcomes, the teacher may use cues, prompts and/or reinforcers to help the student participate in the classroom activities. For the first step, *upon entering the room, respond to teacher's greeting and question in Spanish*, the teacher may provide instructional support that might look like the following:

As each student enters the room, the teacher:

- extends her hand for the student to shake (visual cue)
- says *"Buenos dias, Señor/Señorita ____"* (verbal cue)

If the student responds appropriately (*"Buenos dias, Señora Ames"*), the teacher:

- smiles, says *"Muy bien"* (visual and verbal reinforcer)

If the student is new or has responded incorrectly, the teacher:

- places the student's hand in her hand to shake (physical prompt)
- after giving a greeting, states "say, *'Buenos dias, Señora Ames'*" (verbal prompt)

Understanding these elements of instruction and observing how educators relay information to their students can assist planning teams when a learner is not able to participate in classroom activities at the same level as his/her classmates. Sometimes learners with diverse abilities will require additional or alternative instructional approaches to understand what the expected performance is within any given activity. Some students may only require adjustments to the way instructional information is provided, such as through written instructions along with verbal cues, or by increasing the number of times during the activity a student is given feedback. Additionally, other students may require modifications to the way they perform the activity. Therefore, the next step in an ecological assessment is to evaluate how the student performs the steps of the activity in comparison to classmate performance.

Step 4:

Observe and determine the learner's ability to achieve typical learner outcomes

1. **Can the student achieve the typical learner outcomes without assistance?**
2. **Can the student achieve the typical learner outcomes with additional support?**
3. **Will a different learner outcome be expected for the student in order to participate during the curricular activity?**
4. **If the planning team has determined that the student cannot participate meaningfully in the curricular activity (even wtih a different learner outcome), is an alternative activity/environment needed?**

Student-centered teams will need to assess whether or not the learner with diverse abilities can achieve the expected outcomes of the activity or routine with or without additional support. When students cannot demonstrate mastery of the typical outcome, with appropriate adaptations, additional outcomes identified during the student-centered planning process should be infused into the regular curricular activities when possible. The process of analyzing a student's performance in relation to other classmates is called Discrepancy Analysis (Falvey, Brown, Lyon, Baumgart, & Schroeder, 1980). The planning team identified the typical learner outcomes in Step Three; now the team members must observe the focus student participating in the curricular activity to determine:

1. the steps of the curricular activity the learner can perform independently

If the student cannot perform all or some of the steps of the curricular activity, then...

2. the steps of the curricular activity the learner can perform with a different level and/or type of cue, prompt, or reinforcer in order to achieve the learner outcomes

3. the steps of the curricular activity the learner can perform with different materials or with minimal physical assistance in order to achieve the learner outcomes

If the student is not able to perform the curricular activity to achieve the typical learner outcomes with appropriate adaptations, it will be necessary to either:

✐ alter the learner outcome for the focus student so that he/she can participate in the curricular activity, or

✐ provide a different curricular activity in the same or different learning environment at this time

Let's go back to the example of our middle school Spanish class. Think of a student who may not verbally communicate but who can use an augmentative communication system to speak with classmates and teachers. Although that student is not able to do the steps of the classroom routine/activity as is, he/she may be able to shake the teacher's hand and push the correct keys on the communication system which has been programmed with a Spanish vocabulary to greet the teacher. A learner with more significant needs who cannot verbalize and who has not learned to use an alternative communication method, may be able to shake the teacher's hand, thus, expressing acknowledgment of the teacher's greeting in a different way, though the classroom routine remains the same.

For students who have significantly diverse learning abilities and support needs, it will be important for teams to remember that a student can benefit from class participation in an array of ways. Adjusting expectations about what the student with diverse abilities will learn and how they will demonstrate that learning can maximize the benefits of student involvement within their classroom. Additionally, there are many functional skill areas naturally addressed within the context of curricular activities. Therefore, where students cannot perform the curricular activity to achieve the expected outcomes or to achieve outcomes individualized for that student, student-centered planning teams will need to problem-solve the ways in which a student's educational needs can be addressed within the same or alternative curricular activity/environment.

Appendix D, the *Student Observation Form*, is a recording sheet which teams may find useful to:

1. identify typical learner outcomes and steps in classroom routines/activities,
2. determine how the learner performs the curricular activities to achieve the typcial learner outcomes, and
3. brainstorm possible suggestions for adaptations, supports or individualized learner outcomes when necessary.

Table III illustrates the use of this environmental assessment by Phillip's planning team. Where Philip is unable to perform the steps of the curricular activities to achieve the typical outcomes, alternative curricular activities have been considered. The team now has the information necessary to develop individualized learner outcomes.

Student Observation Form

Student's Name: Phillip **Class:** Mathematics **Teacher:** Mr. Ford

Typical Learner Participation	Student Participation	Possible Adaptations or Alternative Activities	Phillip's Learner Outcomes
1. Copy and compute 5 review math problems from overhead.	Tries to copy numbers but reverses number order; only copies two problems, writing addition sign rather than multiplication sign; uses several lines on paper to write problem; begins to add numbers using fingers to count; rewrites first problem.	• provide an enlarged xerox of overhead • have Phillip choose and circle two problems he will copy and solve; • bold line paper, staring with a larger writing area, decreasing as he stays within boundaries • have Phillip identify addition, subtraction, and multiplication functions; verbalize which function to use in problem; use calculator to solve problem applying correct function	• choose two problems; copy onto paper and solve with peer assistance • use calculator to solve addition and subtraction problems
2. Demonstrate cooperative group skills when practicing mastered content skills	• Can show peer flashcard with answers written on back; • can determine if answer is correct if classmates respond by giving each digit separately; e.g., 24 is stated as "number 2 and number 4." • When answering, can say one-digit numbers if prompted by classmates; does not know function sign, tried to add numbers using fingers instead of multiplying or dividing.	• use calculator and appropriate function to determine answer from flashcard • increase two-digit number identification • verbalize number when shown two-digit number flashcards • enlarge print on flashcards • color code function to assist in recognition	• demonstrates knowledge of function sign (addition, subtraction, multiplication) by telling classmate which is appropriate • learns to recognize and say two-digit numbers appropriately
3. Participate in class discussion of next-level skill information 4. Compute practice problem from board with modeling	• Attends to teacher for several minutes • Begins to play with pencil, starts to tap pencil on the head of the classmate in front of him • Teacher tells Phillip to put pencil down and look at book • Phillip continues to tap peer on head • Teacher takes pencil away • Phillip puts head down for the remainder of whole-group instruction	• ask peer for assistance when needed to find appropriate page/problem • teacher will alternate asking Phillip questions about numbers/functions on board with pointing to problem/numbers • partner with peer for assistance in following in book • use the last ten minutes of the review period to use telephone in office. • once a week, learn about a mathematically-related career and share information with classmates	• will increase attention to teacher through question answering • will follow teacher's directions to work with peer on practice problem • increase use of calculator to solve next-level practice problems • practice telephone skills in office during testing periods

Table III

Step 5:

Identify individualized learner outcomes which reflect the curricular content focus and the learner's life-long goals and instructional needs

The final step in this systematic assessment process is to problem-solve alternative outcomes students can demonstrate which will:

✎ maximize participation in the classroom activities and routines

✎ assist teams to identify specifically how a student will demonstrate the needed skills within the context of the curricular activity

✎ allow educators to report progress based on individual performance

✎ value the student as a learner within the classroom

Recall the discussion regarding the development of learner outcomes from page 3 of this manual. Learner outcomes create the framework to define the necessary student performance for successful accomplishment of the course or curricular objectives.

Learner outcomes also provide a vehicle for educators to determine grading criteria. Some students with diverse learning abilities may not be capable of demonstrating achievement of these learner outcomes in the same way. However, these students can benefit from typical curricular activities when outcomes are adjusted to allow for different learning needs. It will be up to the educational team to come to agreement on which outcomes are then used to provide grades, and what percentages/weight will be appropriate for each outcome in determining the final grade for the student (Figure 7).

Individualized learner outcomes emerge when student needs are infused with skills which aid learners in the performance of curricular activities in the same, similar, or alternative manner as their classmates. As with typical outcomes, individualized learner outcomes allow educators to monitor student achievement in the skill areas related to their needs and determine grading based on progress toward these outcomes. Furthermore, individual learner outcomes can serve as a foundation in the development of goals and objectives in the learner's

individualized educational program (IEP). When developing individualized learner outcomes, teams will want to consider the following questions:

✎ Are there skill areas which have been previously identified as needs for the learner that relate to the typical classroom outcomes?

✎ Will a different skill allow the student to demonstrate the learner outcomes in a different manner?

✎ Are there skills the student has mastered which can be enhanced to assist them in meeting the typical learner outcome?

✎ Based on the previously identified needs, will an alternative activity which relates to the curricular content better maximize the student's participation?

Remember our example of the student with significantly diverse needs in the Spanish class at the middle school level. Although, in all probability, this learner will not demonstrate verbal abilities to speak the Spanish language, she can still benefit from participating in this class

Grading Agreement

Student's Name: Phillip   **Course/Class:** Mathematics
Grade: 4   **Period/Time:** 11:30–12:15
Support Teacher: Ms. Johnson   **Classroom Teacher:** Mr. Ford

Student Learner Outcome for Course	IEP Goal or Objective? Yes No	% of Grade	Measurement	How Often?
Solve two selected problems using a calculator during daily review and tests	X	25%	% accuracy of xerox review worksheet and tests	daily/weekly
Label two-digit numbers on flashcards during cooperative group	X	15%	teacher/peer observation data recording of accuracy by support teacher	daily weekly
Use a calculator to solve flashcard problems and check member answers during cooperative group	X	15%	teacher/peer observation data recording of accuracy by cooperative group members	daily weekly
Correctly dial home telephone number	X	20%	data recording /support teacher	daily during acquisition; weekly upon mastery
Correctly copy three math game problems from a peer's paper	X	25%	% copies correctly on paper	daily

Support or adaptations needed: enlarged Xerox copy of review overhead and weekly tests, bold-lined paper, calculator with color-coded dots for different functions, peer support for assistance with finding correct page when needed, support teacher assistance to office/calling home.

Student

Parent

Classroom/Course Teacher

Support Teacher

Figure 7

by building upon her existing skills as well as developing new ones. For this learner, the student-centered planning team identified several instructional skill areas which could be addressed during the Spanish class. Those skills the team identified which could be infused into the first typical outcome included:

✐ respond to others when interactions are initiated (e.g. greetings, questions, etc.)

✐ learn to use a switch to access technology (e.g. computer, tape recorder, etc.)

Based on the typical learner outcome, which was, *Upon entering the room, respond to the teacher's greeting and question in Spanish,* and the previously identified instructional needs of the student who needed to learn how to use an alternative communication system, the team for this student has identified the following individualized learner outcomes:

✐ orient toward the speaker when his/her name is called

✐ use a switch to activate a tape recorder with a prerecorded greeting on the audiotape

Appendix E, the *Individualized Learner Outcome Matrix,* can be a valuable tool for team members to incorporate to assist with determining where learner needs will be best addressed within the context of the typical curriculum. Table IV illustrates an outcome matrix Phillip's team has designed. Note that each need for skill development and support is attended to within the context of math activities. Additionally, each individualized outcome renders a concise measurement criteria for expected student performance for grading purposes.

Although Phillip is unable to demonstrate the typical learner outcomes as stated to meet the math objectives, he is capable of performing some parts of the activity. Additionally, he can demonstrate some of the skills within the typical learner outcomes with alterations. Currently, given a visual cue, Phillip can identify the function to use in a given problem, and with direct instruction and peer support, he is able to use a calculator to solve simplified math calculations as was determined when his team performed a discrepancy analysis. Table IV reflects the learner outcomes for which Phillip will

be held accountable to demonstrate his achievement of the grade-level curricular content.

Conclusion

A systematic and performance-based assessment model can guide teams in the development of outcomes which are reflective of typical curricular activities but are designed to respect the unique and individual needs of learners with diverse abilities. As schools move toward a vision of inclusive educational services, this process can provide a foundation for adults to collaboratively partner and brainstorm so that every child is valued as a learner in their school community. As schools commit to improving student learning, the success of educating all students will call for new roles for educators and families in creating optimal learning environments for all students, including students with diverse learning needs. Such schools will become purposeful communities which set as a common theme the idea of inclusiveness, "where differences are brought together as part of the common whole" (Sergiovanni, 1994).

Phillip's Individualized Learner Outcome Matrix

Instructional and/or Support Need	Individualized Learner Outcome	Instructional and/or Support Need	Individualized Learner Outcome
respond to greetings	• verbally greet teacher	answer questions	• given a visual cue, respond to teacher questions during classroom discussion
make choices	• select and circle two problems to solve during independent review	identify/write numbers	• increase two-digit number identification and verbalize number when shown a two-digit number flashcard • copy and solve two problems, using a calculator, for independent review • copy three math games problems from a peer's paper and solve using a calculator
follow directions	• comply within a five-second period when given direction from the teacher	use telephone	• dial the sequence of numbers necessary to call home
ask/accept assistance	• ask peer for assistance when needed to find appropriate page/problem	use a calculator	• identify addition, subtraction, multiplication and division functions and use correct function on calculator to solve problem • use a calculator and appropriate function to determine the answer to independent review problems, check peer answers to flashcards, solve three game problems, and to complete at least five homework problems.
follow routine	• use a picture schedule to prepare for upcoming activities	copy letters/numbers from model	• choose and copy two review problems from xeroxed overhead • copy three math game problems from peer paper • copy homework assignment from board onto notebook paper
work cooperatively with peers	• assist peers in checking answers using a calculator • partner with peer to assist with following in book.	learn about jobs	• together with parents, gather information about a mathematically-related career and share in class

Table IV

References

Armstrong, T. (1994). *Multiple intelligences in the classroom*. Alexandria, Virginia: The Association for Supervision and Curriculum Development.

Bellamy, T. G. (1993). *The whole school framework: A guide for systemic school-level reform (draft)*. Paper submitted for publication. Denver, Colorado, University of Colorado at Denver.

Brown, L., Branston, M. B., Hamre-Nietupski, S. Pumpian, I., Certo, N., & Gruenwald, L. (1979). A strategy for developing chronological age appropriate and functional curricular content for severely handicapped adolescent and young adults. *Journal of Special Education, 13*(1), 81–90.

Colorado School Laws (1994). The Colorado Standards-Based Education Law. CRS 22-53-401 to 22-53-410. Denver, Colorado: Colorado Department of Education.

Donnelan, A., Mirenda, P., Mesaros, R., & Fassbender, L. (1984). Analyzing the communicative functions of aberrant behavior. *The Journal of the Association of Persons with Severe Handicaps, 9*(3), 201–212.

Falvey, M., Brown, L., Lyon, S., Baumgart, D., & Schroeder, J. (1980). Strategies for using cues and correction procedures. In W. Sailor, B. Wilcox, & L. Brown (Eds.), *Methods of instruction for severely handicapped students*. Baltimore: Paul H. Brookes Publishing Co.

Falvey, M.A., Forest, M., Pearpoint, J., & Rosenberg, R. (1994). Building connections. In J. Thousand, R. Villa & A.I. Nevin (Eds.), *Creativity & Collaborative Learning*. Baltimore: Paul H. Brookes Publishing Co.

Giangreco, M. F. (1992). Curriculum in inclusion-oriented schools: Trends, issues, challenges, and potential solutions. In S. Stainback & W. Stainback (Eds.). *Curriculum Considerations in inclusive classroom: Facilitating learning for all students*. Baltimore: Paul H. Brookes Publishing Co. Haring, T.G., & Lovinger, L. (1989). Promoting social interaction through teaching generalized play initial responses to preschool children with autism. *The Journal of the Association for Persons with Severe Handicaps, 14*(1), 58–67.

Maslow, A.H. (1968). *Toward a psychology of being*. New York: D. Van Nostrand Co.

Mount, B. (1987). *Personal futures planning: Finding directions for change*. Unpublished doctoral dissertation, University of Georgia.

National Council on Education Standards and Testing (January 24, 1992). *Raising Standards for American Education*. Washington, D.C.: Author.

Roggow, R. & Rogers-Connolly, T. (1992). *Individualized Planning Sessions (IPS): A statewide initiative for enhancing the quality of life for individuals with special needs*. Paper presented at the National Association for Persons with Severe Handicaps Conference, San Francisco.

Sergiovanni, T. (1994). *Building community in schools*. San Francisco: Jossey-Bass Publishers.

Tashie, C., Shapiro-Barnard, S., Schuh, M., Jorgenson, C., Dillon, A., and Nisbet., J. (1993). *From special to regular, from ordinary to extraordinary*. Durham, N.H.: Institute on Disability/UAP, University of New Hampshire.

Udvari-Solner, A. (1992). *Curricular adaptations: Accommodating the instructional needs of diverse learners in the context of general education*. Topeka: Kansas State Board of Education.

Villa R. & Thousand, J. (1991). Administrative supports for educating all children in the mainstream of regular education. In S. Stainback & W. Stainback (Eds.), *Supports for educating all children in the mainstream of regular education*. Baltimore: Paul Brookes Publishing.

Appendices

Checklist for Identifying Student Support and Instructional Needs within Regular Education Classrooms

Communicative Needs	Behavior/Affective Needs	Physical Needs	Relationship Needs
❏ The student has access to usable and portable communication methods and/or systems. ❏ Assessment of the student's communication needs is based on typical routines and activities within the classroom as well as classmate input ❏ The teacher and classmates are aware of and understand the communication methods used by the student ❏ Direct instruction in use of the student's communication method/system is in place ❏ Opportunities exist for the student to practice and use the communication method/system within the classroom.	❏ Teacher proximity to the student during instruction allows for effective behavior management. ❏ The level of prompting and reinforcement the learner requires to maintain successful performance is understood and used across classroom activities. ❏ Self-management techniques, including self-directed goal setting and self-montoring of behaviors, are used in conjunction with or as an alternative to the typical classroom management strategies. ❏ Instruction to the learner integrates the use of social skills and replacement behaviors. ❏ The teacher understands and uses redirective techniques. ❏ There are choices presented within activities. ❏ Activities of interest, ability, and motivation for the student are available.	❏ The student's mobility assistance within the classroom and throughout the school has been assessed and the appropriate supports and modifications provided. ❏ The teacher and classmates are aware of the student's physical activity requirements and allow for those needs during the classroom routine (e.g., standing at desk area to complete work, repositioning in wheelchair). ❏ The student's physical ability to manipulate materials and technology has been assessed and the appropriate modifications have been provided. ❏ The teacher and classmates understand how to use the modified technology with the student. ❏ The student's workspace needs have been assessed and modified. ❏ Classmates have been trained to provide safe mobility assistance to the student.	❏ The student has a method of communicating with peers. ❏ The teacher and peers are aware of how to interact with the student. ❏ There are naturally occurring opportunities for the student to interact with classmates. ❏ The staff is aware of the least intrusive methods to facilitate interaction between the student and his/her classmates. ❏ There are opportunities for the student to engage in preferred activities with classmates. ❏ The teacher and classmates are aware of the student's special talents and provide opportunities for the student to demonstrate those skills.

Appendix A

Checklist for Identifying Student Support and Instructional Needs within Regular Education Classrooms—con't.

Time Management Needs	Personal Care and Organization Needs	Academic Needs	Life-Skill Needs
❏ The student is provided with the lead time or peer assistance needed to move about the school within the alloted timeframes. ❏ The student can self-monitor time allotments for specified activities or is provided with the support to cue management. ❏ The student has a written or picture schedule of daily activities, when necessary. ❏ The educational staff and classmates are aware of cues (verbal, pictoral, gestural) to be provided to the the student as necessary to prepare for transition times.	❏ Accessible personal care facilities (drinking fountains, restrooms, specified areas for personal protection changes) are located near the classroom. ❏ Educational staff and classmates understand the student's methods of communicating personal care needs. ❏ Educational staff are aware of the student's scheduled personal care needs, if different from the typical personal care schedule of the classroom. ❏ Availability of resources within the building that support students in personal assistance needs (eating, toileting, dressing, etc.) has been identified. ❏ Educational staff and classmates are aware of any medical needs of the student and have information and training from the school nurse, as appropriate. ❏ The student has access to a physically-accessible locker or cubby . ❏ The student's school supplies are tabbed and labeled, as appropriate.	❏ The teacher and classmates are aware of and understand the student's method and ability to comminicate information related to academic learning . ❏ Educational staff provide opportunities for the student to use information related to academic learning in applied situations in daily life. ❏ Educational staff are aware of the student's ability to generalize academic information from setting to setting and provide the necessary modifications to ensure skill application. ❏ The teacher is aware of the student's motivation and interest in the different academic content areas and provide instructional activities based on this information.	❏ The educational staff is aware of the student's and his/her family's lifelong goals in the areas of career, domestic recreation and community involvement. ❏ The educational staff has determined areas in which the student will require support to participate in regular classroom activities that focus on the skills necessary to achieve these lifelong goals. ❏ The teacher and classmates are aware of the student's interests and abilities. ❏ The teacher and classmates understand that the student can partially participate in activities which he/she is not capable of doing independently. ❏ The educational staff provide opportunities for the student to self-advocate for choices and assistance needs.

Appendix A-2

Appendix B

Daily Schedule/Student Needs
Classroom Schedule

Instructional and Support Needs

Classroom Analysis

Class/Course: _____ Teacher:_____Time/Period:_____ Room Number: _____

What are the curricular outcomes for this class?	What is the teaching format/instructional grouping arrangement?	What are common routines/classroom management techniques?
What learning materials are used?	**How are grades assigned?**	**What collaboration/support needs might the teacher want?**

Student Observation Form

Student's Name: _____ Class: _____ Teacher: _____ Date of Observation:_____

Class Routine/Curricular Sequence	Student Level of Participation	Possible Support Needs/Individualized Learner Outcome

Appendix E

Learner Outcome Matrix

Student: _____   Subject: _____

Instructional/ Support Need	Learner Outcome	Support Need	Learner Outcome
1.	•	7.	•
2.	•	8.	•
3.	•	9.	•
4.	•	10.	•
5.	•	11.	•
6.	•	12.	•